WORKPLACE UTOPIA

MEDITATIONS ON CREATING AN ACTIVELY
ENGAGED, HAPPY, RELAXED, HIGHLY
PRODUCTIVE WORK ENVIRONMENT. THIS
BOOK IS FOR MANAGERS WITH A GROWTH
MINDSET.

DAVID E FERRERS

COACH HOUSE PUBLISHING

Copyright

Other books by David Ferrers

Personal Development:

Ignite Your Inner Leader

A Journey of Self-Discovery

The Achievers - with David Norton

Create The Life You Want

SWAP

Novels:

The Hero of Hastings

Annie's Gift

FOREWARD

There is a world wide Engagement at Work crisis.

Gallup surveys tell us that in every surveyed country in the world only 13% of workers are engaged at work. That means that only 13% of people are giving all they have got to their employers.

I call this a crisis because it affects overall productivity and it suggests that the human creativity essential to our continued progress and prosperity is not flowing through the veins of our business corporations.

Most of the cures being suggested and implemented to attempt to rectify the engagement issue start in the middle or lower echelons of the corporate world. This means that people are being "told" to become more engaged by people who want change but have little intention of changing their own behaviour.

The cure needs to start at the top.

Unless corporate directors recognise the need for change and determine that such change must start with changes in their own behaviour, no change programme will ever gain the credence and traction necessary to create a work environment in which employees become actively engaged with their work.

The purpose of this book is to get you thinking about what you can do about the worldwide work engagement problem. Your prize for creating a stimulating and enjoyable workplace is actively engaged, loyal employees and thus greater productivity.

I am not attempting to write a book full of facts and wise information on how to do it. Neither will there be many stories about how others have done it, because there is a great lack of such stories. My purpose is not to create a template for you, but rather to stimulate your thinking as the precursor to you making radical changes that will lead to the creation of a workplace where all employees are actively engaged.

I am dyslexic. There may well be spelling mistakes or grammar mistakes in the pages that follow. I don't apologise for these because this is the way I am. But because I am dyslexic there will also be different ways of viewing a global issue that urgently needs new thinking.

My motivation is simply to help the millions of people all over the world who are not being provided with a work environment in which they can express themselves and enjoy their work. They are simply wage slaves. I have coached hundreds of such people over the past 25 years. These people have persistently been hindered by workplace environments that fail them. Environments that are uninspiring, that are filled with constant interruptions, that are threatening rather than enthralling.

My approach to dealing with the work environment issue is to ask one simple question: "what changes when a normal, energetic person who is dedicated to creating a happy, loving and secure home comes to work?"

I first started to think this way when considering telephone help lines. I could imagine a very ordinary, sociable human being with a partner and two children answering their telephone at home in a lively and helpful way. Then that same person comes to work in a call centre and suddenly transforms into an obstructive, unhelpful automaton, why?

Something happens to people when they come to work. They seem to feel that they need to behave in ways that conform to some imagined view of expected behaviour. Maybe they have seen movies or TV shows where managers are portrayed in a certain way and they feel that "this is how I need to behave." Or maybe they are simply copying the behaviour of parents or school teachers or their boss. Whatever their role model the result is that at work they morph into someone that they are not.

Trying to be someone that you are not is very stressful. And once a person feels stressed their behaviour becomes erratic, they start to behave in ways that are not their normal, natural behaviour; their productivity declines.

As a result of people not behaving naturally at work, but rather adopting a workplace persona, most people are not happy at work.

My observations are supported by a wealth of statistics that show:

* Only 13% of employees worldwide are engaged. This figure has remained static for over 15 years. (Source: Gallup)

* Disengaged workers have 37% higher absentee rates and are likely to make 60% more errors. (Sources: Queens School of Business & Gallup)

* Actively disengaged employees are reckoned to cost the U.S. economy up to $550 billion a year in lost productivity. (source: Gallup)

Conversely there are statistics that show that:

* Productivity in organisations where employees are connected improves by 20%- 25%. (Source: The McKinsey Global Institute)

* In teams where employee engagement is high productivity rises by 21%. (Source: Gallup)

* In organisations where employee engagement was high the average 3-year revenue growth has been shown to be 2.3 times greater than in organisations where employee engagement was only average. (Source: UNC Kenanflager Business School)

With such a well known problem and such high rewards for solving the problem why has nothing moved in the past 15 years?

It is time to make changes.

Pause & Meditate on: *What can I do to improve my organisation's engagement issue?*

1. THE ISLAND

I magine that you have just been marooned on an island with six other people.

You have been there for only a short while when you appreciate that everyone is feeling lost and suffering from self-pity. The group has no direction and morale is low.

Not knowing how long is might be before you are rescued you appreciate the need for shelter and sustenance.

You have no practical skills that might aid survival, but you do have some management experience, so you decide that you can best help the group by getting them organised for survival. You gather everyone together for a situation appreciation session. By asking a few simple questions you ascertain that in your group you have: an amateur carpenter, a chef, someone who fishes for a hobby, an interior designer, a keen amateur gardener and a geologist.

The group agrees to divide into two teams, the carpenter, interior designer and geologist will erect a shelter - the chef, the gardener and fisherman will forage for food.

Now that people have decided what to do you appreciate that you do not have the skills to tell them how to do their jobs. The best way you can be useful is by encouraging, fostering a lively atmosphere and providing a forum to discuss how problems might be solved.

Compare the behaviour of the leader in this situation, with the leader behaviour seen everyday in most corporations.

Notice that basically there is nothing to be gained by constantly asking, "how's it going?" that only serves to interrupt and annoy people. There is no benefit to creating time pressure, everyone is aware that shelter and sustenance are needed. Everyone knows that the benefits will come when the tasks are completed in the best way possible in the minimum of time, they don't have to be told or harried. Quality and timeliness are in their best interests.

Pause & Meditate on: *How would I behave on an island like this? How would I encourage people to give of their best?*

2. WORKPLACE UTOPIA

What is workplace Utopia like?

Everyone is beavering away at their work. They are obviously enjoying their activities. They are highly productive and feel proud of their achievements. They are a committed and highly loyal workforce.

What is meditation?

You sit calmly and think. Your mind is focussed on a single subject. You go on and on thinking about the subject until a good answer is revealed to you.

Meditation is *not* about forcing a solution to appear from your conscious mind. It is *not* about studying statistics and case histories and then copying what others do. It *is* about being relaxed and allowing your inner voice to tell you what is right for you to do, right now.

"Do not tell me it can't be done."

Franklin D. Roosevelt

3. HOW DO PEOPLE BEHAVE WHEN THEY'RE AT THEIR BEST

Most people are at their best when they're attending a social gathering; at a party or a family get-together.

Imagine yourself at a social gathering. Look around at the other people and notice:

* most people are *smiling*.

* People are *conversing easily* with one another.

* People are *being solicitous*, they are taking an active interest in one-another's wellbeing.

* They all look *relaxed*.

* Notice how people of all ages, occupations and status converse easily with one another. There is no ordering about, no bossiness.

* Notice how guests *offer to help* the host and hostess. Or, when they're asked, how people *willingly help* the host and hostess.

* Notice the high level of *natural energy* in the room and how it flows.

* Notice that people are *sharing helpful information*, possibly about car insurance deals, or where to buy plants, or about good holiday locations.

* Notice the *sharing of small gifts* like food and drink.

* Notice also the *lack of interruptions* from smart phones. The people are being together with one another not with their phones.

Now, compare the behaviour of this group of naturally social-ising people with the normal everyday behaviour that you witness in your work environment.

Pause & Meditate on: *What do I have to do to create this kind of enjoyable, relaxed, lively, cooperative environment where I work?*

4. WHERE DO PEOPLE GIVE OF THEIR BEST?

I n this chapter we're considering the sorts of environments where people behave with high energy and where they cooperate and coordinate together.

The two environments that spring instantly to mind are parties and sports arenas. What have these two locations got in common?

At both there is a common purpose - to score. It may be just about impressing someone else or it may be about your team overcoming their opposition. Whichever, there is a definite sense of purpose to the occasion.

There is an often an air of celebration. Maybe it is someone's birthday, or maybe your team wins. But, this is not necessary to the creation of the energy. The sense of purpose is more important than the celebration. It is that sense of purpose that brings people and unites them in the expending of their energy. Even if you are only there to enjoy yourself or to share in the feeling of comradeship, you have a purpose in being there.

Notice that the sense of purpose has to have meaning for each individual. Birthdays have meaning, they are a celebration of the continuity of life. Every team has meaning for its supporters. We put our energy into the occasion.

Pause & Meditate on: *Is there a uniting sense of purpose where I work? What can I do to help create meaning and a sense of purpose at work?*

5. LEADERSHIP

Are you a boss or a leader?

The enemies of good leadership are force, command and ego. All too often leaders' egos demand that they be recognised as the top dog. Such attitudes get in the way of open, creative discussion. They want their commands to be implemented. Egos hinder potential synergy. They create an environment where people have to do as they are told. As a result many people feel frustrated because they are not allowed the freedom to express themselves; they feel confined and stressed.

Human beings are not robots (they are coming soon enough). The strengths of the human being are in their originality, their unique library of knowledge and abilities, their creativity and their insights. To mine these talents it is necessary to give the people the space in which to be creative. On top of that people need to be valued and to feel that they are valued, so they need to be listened to.

In his book Good to Great author Jim Collins wanted to find out why some companies can move from being good to being great and sustain that success for at least 15 years. The answer in nearly every case was leadership. But it is not the sort of leadership often portrayed and eulogised in movies and TV shows. Not the dominating, egocentric know it all, hard-driving, always right superhero. Rather the leaders of these sustained successes turned out to be self-effacing, questioning, seekers after improvement.

In my view the greatest words ever written about the art of leadership are these from U.S. President Dwight David Eisenhower:

"Leadership is the art of getting someone else to do what you want done because they want to do it."

Art means, according to the Oxford dictionaries, "the expression or application of human creative skills and imagination."

Pause a moment and consider the place where you work. Ask yourself, "how much 'creative skill and imagination' do I see being exercised by the leaders where I work?"

Someone else to do, ah yes, "I must get them to do." In many leaders' eyes that is the holy of holies. They don't pause to think about the strengths of their fellow workers, all they want is to get them to "do". The leader becomes consumed by results without pausing to give thought to "what is the best way to get this person, with their unique skills and abilities, to do what I want done?"

Leaders should be chosen first for their ability to inspire, second for their ability to organise and lastly for how much they know about the area in which they are to lead. When read these words you have to recognise that the ability to inspire involves listening and learning. The leader who knows it all, or thinks they know it all, is likely to inhibit those reporting to them and dry up the flow of ideas.

Ah, but there isn't time for pausing to think of each individual, I have to get this done by tomorrow.

Think of someone preparing a meal for some special guests who are coming to dinner this evening. They don't have to be told what to do or how to do it. They make their own decisions about what to cook, what ingredients to buy, when to start cooking and how to cook it. The meal appears on the table at the appropriate time. All you had to tell the cook was how many people were coming and what time you want to eat. The cook may have asked about special known likes and dislikes, dietary requirements and budget. They didn't need to be constantly harried and hurried. All they need is encouragement and meaningful offers of help.

Because they want to do it means that you have tapped in to what they like doing and you have connected with that person in such a way that they want to please you. Because of your relationship they take a pride in pleasing you.

When interviewing prospective candidates for a position do you focus primarily on uncovering their work skills to find out if they can do the job, and do you spend an equal amount of time uncovering what they love doing, what gives them a real sense of pride?

It is quite common for people to have developed a fair amount of proficiency at exercising a particular skill simply because that is what they have been taught to do and encouraged to do. But that may not mean that what they are proficient at is their passion. It is only when people are passionate about their subject that they put their heart and soul into their work. Only then are they actively engaged.

Human beings like to please on another. This feeling is the basis of all good service. We want to please and know that we have pleased.

The role of the leader is to transform, themselves, their employees and their organisation constantly. To create an environment in which people want to excel and are able to excel.

Pause & Meditate on: *what is my personal leadership style? Does my leadership style encourage people to want to do what I want done? Do people feel proud and happy when they deliver what I want done? What am I doing to help them to feel that way?*

6. FINDING YOUR IKIGAI, YOUR PASSION

Work can either be a slog or a joy. It becomes a joy when we are given the opportunity to do what we love to do and when we are given the time and environment in which to do it.

When people are constantly doing what they love to do they are actively engaged. They are in utopia.

Ikigai is a Japanese word that roughly translates as "your passion" or "what you leap out of bed to do every morning."

A key question then is, "how do I find my passion, what I love to do?"

You need to open up your whole mind, both your logical left brain and your creative right brain. Then you need to observe yourself. It can help to keep a diary, or a log, in which you note down times when you feel good. What were you doing at those times?

Your notes need to be specific not general. In other words, not, "I was in a meeting and I felt good." But, "During the meeting I spoke about 'encouraging creativity'. I made some useful points and everyone listened attentively." This note would reveal that *encouraging creativity* is something in which you are deeply interested. You must have thought about the subject because you had the background information to "make some good points."

From the above notes you would know that *encouraging creativity* is an important element of your ikigai. What other pieces of your ikigai do you need to find? You might try focussing on *encouraging*, is encouraging other people an important element of who you are. Or, you might focus on *creativity*. Is being creative part of who you are?

As part of your awareness you might notice the times when you are so engrossed in what you are doing that you fail to notice the passing of time. You start to develop a plan for how you will deliver on a project and before you know it two hours have passed and you will be late home that night. But there is useful information in your passionate engagement with the plan you were writing. The fact that you lost track of time tells you that *planning* is part of your ikigai.

Can you link together *creative* and *planning* into a job that will allow you to express yourself in ways that will satisfy you?

Feedback is designed to tell you how well you have done. It is also a useful way of making you aware of your strengths and weaknesses, your likes and dislikes. When you become more self aware you start to notice what makes you feel good. At the same time you will notice how your performance often improves when you are feeling good. From this position of self awareness you can start to become more aware of what makes other people feel good and how their performance improves when they are feeling a sense of pride in their performance.

But, how do you react to feedback? Do you just think, "they are only telling me that to make me feel less bad about having to do it again?" Or does some feedback offend you and make you withdraw into yourself. Or do you find it more difficult to accept feedback from certain types of people. Or do you just feel warm all over knowing that you have contributed to making another person's life just a little bit better? Your reactions to feedback are vitally important to your ability to make progress.

If praising feedback makes you feel justified, "there I knew I was right all along". Or if critical feedback makes you retreat into yourself or look for someone to blame then you have a fixed mindset that will hinder your progress. If However, you react to feedback by telling yourself, "that's great, I learned something new" or "OK, so that doesn't work, I must find another way and try harder," then you have a growth mindset and you will find your ikigai.

It is not always pleasant to be told that your performance has been substandard, but it is vital to know the truth about your performance so that you can understand your likes and dislikes and take action to improve. There will be more on feedback in a later chapter.

Pause & Meditate on: *what do I really love doing? What feedback gives me a real buzz? What am I doing when I lose track of time? What activities make me feel good?*

7. THE RIVER OF EMOTION

I t is true to say that everyone in any position of authority in any organisation got there because of either their ability to do things or to get other people to do things.

The questions are; "in what way do they get people to do things?" And, "how do people feel when they are asked/told to do things?"

Every organisation is powered by a river of emotion that flows through its people.

The word "emotion" is derived from the latin "emovere" meaning "to set in motion." It is your emotions that set your mind in motion. Bad feelings like anger and discontent lead to harmful thoughts. Good feelings like happiness and pride lead to positive thoughts and actions.

Your feelings condition your mind and create your view of the world. When you feel good the world is a bed of roses, when you feel bad you become lethargic or negative and the whole world is against you.

When the waters of the river of emotion in a workplace are choppy production goes down. When the water flows oily smooth productivity goes up.

The waters are disrupted by disgruntlement. They are smoothed by work satisfaction.

The job of the leader is to get done what they want done in ways that allows people to feel satisfaction with what they have done.

The waters become choppy when leaders start to feel concerned and under pressure. As their concerns grow they can start to feel that they have to do more to make things happen. Then they can start to interfere, to micro manage. They might then organise more meetings, send out more emails, make more phone calls. This starts to eat up the time of those trying to get the work done. They spend more time in meetings, more time answering emails and, as they have less and less time to get on with their work, their job satisfaction declines.

Of course there will always be pressure in the workplace. Pressure created by the need to make money. But the moment that making money becomes the centre of attention the whole organisation starts to stress. It is only when the focus is on quality of output that people can start to take pride in what they are doing. Once self-expression and pride enter the river of emotion you are onto a winner.

Whoever felt proud that their organisation made an extra million dollars of profit last year? The workers never see any of that extra million dollars, it mainly gets swallowed up by shareholders and directors.

But imagine the pride of workers who produced the first

award winning iPhone and saw it become a game-changing world beater. Or those who produced the first Tesla, all-electric car. Or those who worked for the airline where the boss turned up to personally greet their customers; that must have told everyone that there was great satisfaction with the quality of the service they gave.

If feedback is only related to quantitative output it usually becomes sterile and slows the flow of the river. However when feedback is related to quality of output, and the skill and effort put into the creation of that quality people find the feedback meaningful and inspiring. This is because they can then recognise that the part they played in achieving the result added value and they feel proud of their achievement.

In a hockey team only one player scores the goal but all the players share in the delight because they all contributed to the creation of the quality movement that made possible the scoring of the goal. The same feeling of delight can be experienced in the workplace.

The problems that prevent the feeling of delight in any organisation are usually embedded in its history, the behaviour of its people and the bad habits that have become embedded in their ways of operating.

When there is a history of command style management, the people at the top got there by commanding others. They continue in that style because it has proved an effective way for them to climb the corporate ladder. Ambitious others see that style succeeding so they copy it and the cycle repeats itself. But gradually the level of dissatisfaction amongst the employees increases and productivity declines no matter how much pressure the leaders exert. Statistics repeatedly show that stress has an adverse effect on performance. There are many case studies of sports people who froze when the sight of the winning post created so much stress that they could not longer remain relaxed and perform. Golfers and footballers get the yips, tennis players loose their serve toss, ice skaters suddenly fall.

When you work closely with individuals within multi-nationals you see this pattern of stress creation over and over again. You also hear the stories of engagement problems constantly. The two are surely linked.

So can habits be changed. We know that people manage to kick their addiction to even the most addictive of substances like tobacco, alcohol and hard drugs. But the transition is always painful and time consuming; it takes clear goals, motivation and hard work.

In an organisation the challenge is even greater because it is not just one person who needs to change but a whole team of people.

In my view you cannot change a whole group of people by the simple announcement that you are going to change, the top manager has to lead the change and they have to lead by example. In order to do this the leader has to be consistently behaving like this:

* Develop and hold a clear vision of how everyone in the organisation should behave. The focus being on creating a workplace where positive emotions flow so that everyone feels good.

* Constant training and practice at behaving in ways that encourage a flow of positive emotion and the development of growth mindsets.

* Constant performance measurement via daily feedback about performance and how it is impacting the rest of the workforce.

Pause & Meditate on: *The advantages of creating a happy workplace where positive emotions flow and people are enjoying their work.*

Visualise your workplace when everyone looks happy and is energetically and purposefully going about their business.

8. MINDSETS

I am indebted to Professor Carol Dweck of Stanford University for her leadership in the field of mindsets.

In the last chapter I discussed habits and how they can hold back productivity when they become ingrained in corporate behaviour. Equally good habits can become ingrained and they can revolutionise corporate behaviour.

Over the years I have become convinced that people do not like to think too much. They are happy to fantasise and to imagine what they might do, without commitment; but they find thinking to be hard work and often seek ways to avoid thinking.

My suspicion is that we become set in our ways because it is easier to be that way, it is easier to be on autopilot than to have to constantly pause and review the "what" and "why" of your behaviour. It makes us feel more secure and because we can join a "clan" of other people who think and behave in the same way - it's cosy that way. The fact that human beings are tribal animals means that we like to join up with other like-minded people to share similar thoughts and ideas; joining such groups makes us feel more secure.

Living with a fixed mindset saves us a lot of thinking bother and makes us feel safer. However, it is also a very threatening state of mind. When something happens that shows us to be wrong about a previously held belief it can be a shattering experience. The company director who always believed himself to be fair-minded becomes confused and upset when he is portrayed as being selfish and bigoted. He looks for someone or something to blame for this apparent anomaly. The head of product testing who always saw herself as rigorous is shattered when the basis of her research turns out to be flawed. She suddenly feels lost because the foundation of her self-confidence has been undermined. She looks for someone or something to blame for this apparent anomaly.

When we hold a certain inflexible self-image and strong beliefs we will defend them strongly. But when they are undermined a foundation of our very life is removed and our whole self-belief structure becomes shaky. We start to doubt ourselves and to lose faith in the structure of knowledge and beliefs on which we have built our security.

The fears of undermining our self-image and our beliefs are strong contributors to our dislike of change. If we change one thing, will it undermine something else?

Company directors find it easy to believe that they are worthy of huge salaries and bonuses whilst paying low wages to employees. They can justify such beliefs by telling themselves that they are better qualified and that they have worked hard for their position and their rewards. With their fixed mindsets it bothers them little that many of their employees cannot afford decent housing and that they get themselves in to debt simply because they are trying to live enjoyable lives.

But what actually happens when directors adopt a growth mindset? What happens when senior managers say to themselves, "the way things are is unsustainable. Most of our employees are not engaged in their work. They are not getting any job satisfaction, they are not expressing themselves; therefore they are not giving us they best of what they have to give. We have to change the work environment, to provide a workplace where people can be, and want to be more productive." In fact they have to admit, "fundamentally we're going about this in the wrong way."

Scary.

But consider this: your mind is nothing more than a stream of thoughts and experiences. You can do with them what you will.

So can major change be achieved? Are there precedents?

In the mid eighties IBM was king of the personal computer world. The IBM strategy of buying components and simply assembling them into a box with an IBM badge worked wonderfully well for a while. But then others started to do the same thing, only cheaper, and soon the market was awash with clones. Clinging to the fixed mindset that "this is what we do best", in 1993 IBM posted the then largest corporate loss in history. The massive shock electrified IBM thinking - they had to innovate or go under. With incredible bravery they abandoned their core PC hardware market and, under the leadership of Lou Gerstner they started to question everything - they adopted a growth mindset, they refocussed on IT expertise.

What IBM did was change from their fixed mindset "we make PCs" to a growth mindset, "where is there opportunity for us and how do we capitalise on it?"

Was this a risky strategy? Yes. Did they have a choice? No.

What is interesting is that IBM are not exceptional. Nearly all major corporations have changed substantially throughout their history.

Nokia started out as a paper mill near the town of Nokia. In time they were joined by a manufacturer of rubber tyres and boots. Then they were joined by a cable company. In time they started to make radios, phones and car phones; eventually they focussed on cell phones. Where next?

The Indian IT services company Wipro which earns billions of dollars annually from IT outsourcing and software engineering started out as Western India Vegetable Products selling vegetable oil to Indian housewives.

The lessons from these case studies, and thousands more, is that corporations have to adapt to market trends; they have to be flexible enough to notice and take advantage of opportunities. Or to put it another way, "healthy corporations adapt to changing environments. They recognise that evolution is an inevitable part of life."

The more important lesson is that major changes can be achieved, often with great success, provided the leaders are courageous and have a growth mindset.

The evidence of dissatisfied workforces is plain to see. So why isn't action being taken? Why aren't major changes happening in workplaces around the world?

A major reason is probably that those at the top have little or no incentive to change. They are doing all right. They have huge pay packets. They receive large bonuses. Why would they bother to change a system that rewards them for doing what they are doing now? If everything goes pear shaped they know that they will walk away with a massive payoff. Who cares about the thousands who will lose their jobs and the pensions for which they have given their working lives?

Yuk! Anyone who thinks like this should be pilloried. Where is their sense of responsibility?

Beware irresponsible and selfish directors, the workforce is now better educated than ever before. People's expectations are higher than at any time in history. The opportunities for individuals are richer and more diverse than at any time than they have ever been.

In 2017 the number of new start-up businesses in the UK reached 660,000 and increase of 9% on the 2015 figure. This means that many of the brightest and many of the most dissatisfied are upping sticks and striking out on their own. Why? Probably because they felt confined where they were working.

At the same time the Economic Times in India is forecasting that the country will be home to 10,500 startups by 2020. This will make India the third largest startup base in the world. Why so many startups?

2017 alone saw more startups in the USA than in the previous four years.

What is happening? Why are so many people branching out on their own? Some will have good ideas that they feel compelled to bring to life. But many startups will simply be the result of workplace dissatisfaction.

This means that many of the best people are leaving the corporate workplace. These are the most valuable people. These are the very people with the growth mindsets that can form the catalyst for change to more dynamic workplaces.

The picture seems to show that the best, most dynamic people, those who will create future growth are leaving the fixed mindset corporations.

Pause & Meditate on: *what am I doing that is making people feel disgruntled at work? Is my fixed mindset creating a sterile environment and driving out the best people? What can I do to develop a personal growth mindset? What can I do to develop a growth mindset in my workplace?*

9. ROBOTS

In many manufacturing industries robots have have revolutionised the landscape. Motor cars are now assembled with very little human intervention. Power plants are increasingly being run by robots which are likely to play increasingly important roles in the inspection of radioactive areas of nuclear power plants.

Many industrial activities are now carried out by robots that are responsible for tasks like welding, assembly, painting, packing, labelling, printing circuit boards, testing and inspecting.

In the home robots can already vacuum, wash floors, wash dishes, clean gutters, open and closing curtains, turn on the TV, mow the lawn and keep the home secure.

In offices a new wave of artificial intelligence is revolutionising back office functions. Routine tasks, document checking and software programming are already being carried out by robots.

Robots may not cause massive unemployment as some

pessimists predict, but they will change the office workplace just as they have changed manufacturing workplaces. Such changes will worry people and make them feel even more insecure.

Increasingly people will look at all the jobs lost to robots in other industries and ask themselves, "what impact will robots have on my job? In what ways do I need to develop in order to maintain my income?"

The main changes will be in the tasks that the human worker has to undertake. Mundane, repetitive tasks will be taken over by robots. Interestingly I have never heard of a single case of a robot being invited to a meeting. Robots are never interrupted by emails, texts or phone calls.

For human beings the future will place greater emphasis on thinking and creating. These are tasks that take time and require blocks of time rather than constantly interrupted time.

It is no longer relevant to discuss whether robots are a good thing or a bad thing. They are increasingly becoming a part of our lives, just as the motor car and the vacuum cleaner have become part of our lives.

The relevant questions are, how do we adapt our behaviour to take advantage of robots? and, what becomes the role of the human being in a world where robots take over many of the repetitive and functional tasks? How do I create a work environment in which people think more and develop really smart ideas?

Pause & Meditate on: *what will increasingly be the functions of the human beings in my organisation? What do we have to provide for these human beings in order for them to deliver what we want of them in the future?*

10. CREATIVITY

I n order to keep up with the competition the crying need is always for "new", it is for innovation, for creativity.

The unique strengths of human beings are our ability to be creative, to think outside of the box and to visualise future scenarios. This is not always easy to do. It requires a desperate need to drive creativity or an environment in which creativity is valued and encouraged.

Thus we are brought back to mindsets. People with fixed mindsets tend to be suspicious of ideas. They might feel exposed because they did not think of it first. They might feel exposed because deep down they know that thinking creatively is not their strong suit. They might feel exposed because they fear change itself which might undermine their strengths and their position.

One of the major challenges to be faced by organisations that want to evolve a creative work environment is: "how do we change or get rid of the fixed mindset people and replace them with growth mindset people?"

A big issue will be that many of the so-called brightest people, those with doctorates and degrees are fixed mindset people. They have built their lives on their ability to pass exams, to show the world that they are "the bright ones - the ones who know the right answers". But these are mainly exams with right or wrong answers. Now the challenge will increasingly be that no one knows what the right answers will be for any given organisation in either the immediate or the long term future.

Since the industrial revolution the world has been focussed on process. The role of people has been to make process happen. But in the future robots will look after much of the process and the humans will be responsible for research, opportunity analysis, innovation and decision making. And we know that people do not generally like to make decisions. There is a serious danger of exposing yourself if you make a wrong decision. But we will need to get better at making good decisions.

An important part of using our creative brains will increasingly be our ability to visualise future opportunities, to see how to take advantage of the opportunities and generate profitable outcomes.

Perhaps the current drive to produce more scientists will need to be replaced by a drive to produce more people with well developed "art" abilities like visualisation and future gazing. Hopefully arts subjects will increasingly regain their perceived value on the educational curricula.

As a young man working in an advertising agency I recall an occasion when we needed a new copywriter. I vividly remember the Creative Director announcing, "I don't want anyone with an English degree. Get me someone who speaks the language of the ordinary housewife."

Pause & Meditate on: *Does my organisation value creativity sufficiently highly? Do I allow sufficient time for people to be inventive about the way that they solve problems? Do I give sufficient consideration to ideas that lack quantitive support and appear to be outside of what I consider to be the norm? Am I guilty of crushing ideas with the weight of logical and statistical arguments?*

11. ADVENTURE

I t is interesting and relevant that children love adventure stories, adults admire those who go out on a limb to free-climb difficult mountains and fee-jump off skyscrapers. Action and adventure movies attract strong box office sales. We love to see others taking risks, but most of us would rather avoid taking risks ourselves.

One sad fact of life is that human beings are addicted to the concepts of safety and security. The insurance industry is founded on these concepts. But, like many other concepts they are valuable only in the right contexts. It is valuable to keep your home and family safe. But a business will stagnate if it focusses too much on safety, it is necessary always to keep moving ahead in order to survive and prosper. The same is true of an individual's career; you must keep learning and growing in order to maintain your value as an employee. The implication here is that we all, both individuals and corporations, need to keep growing in order to keep pace with universal progress.

Growing, in this context, means being aware of our thoughts

and environments, experimenting, learning, adapting and growing. The very act of growing can feel scary, but it also makes us feel alive, vital and valuable.

The good news is that once you accept that life is an adventure, that you take risks everyday as part of living and that there is no such thing as "completely safe", you open up your thinking to being more adventurous.

Of course you may not want to totally accept this line of thinking. You are addicted to the wisdom of saving for a rainy day. You like to justify your decisions with the support of facts, figures and precedents. But there was no precedent for a man walking on the moon. No precedent for the windows computer. No precedent for chains of coffee shops when Starbucks launched. No statistical evidence that Star Wars would be a smash hit movie franchise. None of these products would exist without someone somewhere took a massive risk.

Take comfort; compulsive risk takers tell us that once they plunge into the "scary place" they suddenly find themselves in a state of flow. The fear disappears to be replaced by an "automatic pilot" that takes over and "the voice" that tells them what they should do, instinctively.

The risk takers in extreme sports all have absolutely clear goals, they concentrate 100% on their goal, they pay careful attention to feedback from their immediate environment and they listen carefully to their intuition. They take on challenges that are difficult, but not so difficult that they believe them to be beyond their range of skills.

Clear goals: are all your goals absolutely crystal clear? Do you know why you are heading in this direction? Do you know how the world will change, be better, as a result of your achieving your goal? Are you open to feedback, are you able to accommodate mistakes, are you prepared to constantly alter course, to innovate, to keep pushing forward through the darkness towards the shining beacon of your goal?

In Workplace Utopia the main job of top managers is to set clear goals. To describe their goals in language and visions that are meaningful and inspiring to those who have to do the grunt work to attain those goals. The strategies by which the the goals will be achieved are worked out by those who have to implement those strategies.

Look at the world around you. What do people need, what will they need in twenty years time? When everyone travels in a driverless car, what will they do during their journey? How can that journey be made more enjoyable, more worth-while? Will they just gaze aimlessly at their surroundings? Will they study and if so, what will they study? Will they use the time to take refreshments or enjoy a meal?

Will robots make the world a more sterile place? If so, what will the human beings do for stimulation? How will they get excitement into their lives? What will get their blood racing?

In the future what will be the causes that attract people? What will people get excited about? What will so aggravate people that their blood boils and they feel compelled to take action to eliminate the cause of their upset and replace it with some-thing better?

The world champion racing driver Damon Hill once said: "Through that conflict (with Michael Schumacher), I have done things I would never have done. I have found out more about myself. I feel better about myself for having gone to those extremities, for having dug as deep as I have had to. Our limitations are usually in our minds."

It is only when we challenge ourselves that we find the best of ourselves. It is only by adopting an adventurous attitude that we seek out and rise to challenges. The safe route seldom leads to progress.

Pause & Meditate on: *Am I daring and adventurous? Will I enjoy the adventure towards workplace utopia? What mindset do I need to develop in order to enjoy the world that is coming?*

12. WHAT MUST STOP

The whole system of examination type measurement has to end.

The concept that people need to be in one place for a specific amount of time in order to deliver value is ridiculous. We all have ideas when we are driving our cars, walking the dog, lazing in the bath, reading articles. There is not right place to be creative.

I recall that at one corporation where I was employed I had to produce a weekly timesheet stating the amount of time for which I had worked for each of my clients. My timesheet, and those of most of my colleagues, was a work of fiction. It satisfied the accountants' need for allocating cost, but it said nothing about the value that I had actually delivered.

People should be measured only against their clearly defined and mutually agreed goals. "Was the goal achieved, or not?"

The focus should cease being on quantity. How many meetings did you attend? How many phone calls did you make? How many emails did you respond to?

Down with Command/Blame type questions like: "have you done it yet?" "Where is it?" "Why not?" "When will it be done?" These types of questions lead to pressure, guilt feelings and loss of self belief.

All such questions become redundant when forcing work down through the organisation is replaced by reporting upwards on agreed goals. See chapter on Progress.

If senior managers cease to be responsible for cracking the whip and checking on progress, what will they do with themselves?

Answer 1: There has to be no more cracking of whips. It is just this type of behaviour that is largely responsible for the high levels of demotivation and for the lack of workplace engagement.

Answer 2: senior managers will still be responsible for ensuring that progress is made, but they will not do this by constant demanding. It will be achieved by looking at the regular progress reports passed up to them from below and meeting with their reports to discuss what they, the senior manager can do to help the achievement of the goals. In other words the senior manager becomes an active resource for those below them, rather than a slave driver.

What has to stop is the concept that senior managers are superior people. They are the same as all other people. They may know more, but in the ultimate analysis they are simply another important part of the whole which is the organisation.

In workplace utopia a stop must be put to politics and infighting. These insidious practices undermine the organisation, lead to factions and distract people from the main purpose of the business.

Pause & Meditate on: *Does the way that I work create stress and frustration? In what way could I work so as to create a vital, dynamic, creative workplace?*

13. PROGRESS

G reat organisations are like great trees - they grow from the roots upwards.

It is the roots of the tree that draw in essential water to irrigate and cool the tree. It is the same in organisations, it is the employees that provide refreshment and irrigation for the organisation. They provide the sturdy foundations and secure the organisation when adverse winds blow.

Following the tree analogy, the role of the manager becomes one of helping and creating environments. They are, if you like, the leaves of the tree that, by the process of photosynthesis, convert the energy from sunlight into sugars and starches that become food for the tree. Leaves also provide shade and shelter.

The roles of company directors should be seen in a similar way, as feeders of the tree and providers of shelter beneath which the tree can prosper. Their job is not to force the tree to grow, but rather to provide nutrition.

Think about an organisation in this way. To get a plant to grow you need to water the roots and provide nutrients in the form of fertilisers, both of which are absorbed into the plant via the rots. To kill a plant you spray the leaves with a herbicide with is absorbed through the leaves and down into the roots where it causes the plant to die.

A healthy organisation focuses on feeding its roots, the employees, with the nutrients of learning and inspiration so that it can grow. It allows time for each part of the organisation to develop and achieve it's allotted tasks.

An unhealthy organisation dies when the managers contaminate by placing constant pressure on those striving to grow and achieve.

Growth is fertilised by a cause - a reason to be. This is expressed in the corporate mission. When the mission is inspiring the people become engaged, they are excited, energised, they want to be a part of making the mission a reality. Then they do not work for the pay, they work for the cause.

What is your cause - your reason for existing? This can be to do something better than others do it. With Apple their cause initially was to produce simpler, more intuitive, easier to use computers than Microsoft. They spotted the gap that to make computers universally useable people would not want to learn DOS, they would want to be able to use their PC straight out of the box. These same principles of "simple and intuitive" remain causes for the company to this day.

What is your cause - your reason for existing? This can be to build a better .... Sir James Dyson noticed that conventional vacuum cleaners with bags clogged up, were messy and inefficient. He developed, after some five thousand prototypes, the "G-Force" cleaner that used cyclone technology. Producing better and more efficient machines that benefit lives has remained the company's mission.

What is your cause - your reason for existing? This can be to improve the quality of life for others. This might take the form of a health treatment that saves lives, or it might be a chair that solves the backache problem, or a home for disadvantaged people. The market itself only has to exist, what matters is your mission, your passion and technique for your method of improving the quality of life of others.

What matters is the ability of your organisation to actively engage your employees with your mission by giving them opportunities to express themselves in ways that are meaningful for them. This means that each individual must be employed for their skills, their abilities AND for their unique thinking and ideas. And those thoughts and ideas must be allowed expression, they must be listened to and valued.

Progress will only be made when either there is a revolt by the oppressed employees who can no longer bear the suffering of being stifled by oppressive management, or when directors of organisations start to think and behave in ways that encourage individual growth in order to achieve corporate growth.

It is not enough to make the right noises, in order to achieve change the directors of organisations have to start the process by changing the way that they behave in visible and meaningful ways. This will only ever be possible when directors start to believe passionately in the cause of their organisation.

Pause & Meditate on: *Does my organisation have a cause and is it truly meaningful? Are the people with whom I work passionately engaged with our cause? Do I give people the time and space to achieve their goals?*

14. THE UTOPIAN ROLE OF THE COMPANY DIRECTOR

The company director should be:

* someone who believes passionately in the cause that is the company's reason for existing.

* Someone who sets clear, understandable and inspiring goals.

* Someone who develops inspiring and relevant mission statements.

* Someone who knows and understands the business thoroughly.

* Someone who takes responsibility for the development of all employees.

* Someone who can spot opportunities.

* Someone who cares deeply about the welfare of their workforce.

* Someone who believes that each individual employee has a unique contribution to make.

* Someone who provides opportunities for employees to express themselves.

* Someone who trusts and gives opportunities and responsibility to employees.

* Someone dedicated to creating work environments where people thrive and willingly give of their best.

If you do not fit this description please get out of the way and allow someone who does fit the description to take your place.

In other words Directors set direction - they don't say how to achieve it.

Remember that it was 3M employee Spencer Silver who developed a not very sticky adhesive and his colleague Art Fry who came up with the idea of the Post-It Note. An employee at Boardroom books came up they the idea of reducing the size of their books so that they could be posted more cheaply. You only hear ideas like these if you have created an environment in which people are listened to and encouraged to develop and broadcast their ideas.

It is the most senior managers who must be alert and who must value the thoughts and ideas of all their colleagues.

Notice well that there is no mention of large salaries and share options for directors. No mention of preferential treatment. No mention of deferential treatment. Directors need to earn their stripes and they need to stay in touch with all levels of their organisation.

Yes it takes time to remain in touch with all levels, but if you practice Management by Walking Around you will be in touch. It is noticeable that the directors who transform companies like Lou Gerstner of IBM, Dave Packard of Hewlett Packard and Jack Welch of General Electric spent a great deal of their time visiting their satellite organisations. They wanted to see for themselves what was happening and to hear the ideas of those working at the coal face. This upward communication helped feed them with ideas and informed their decision making.

The first World War provides a classic example of the mayhem that ensues when generals are out of touch with the situation on the battle front. Generals Haig, French and Kitchener were insensitive to the slaughter on the battlefront simply because the mountains of dead soldiers were nothing more to them than mere statistics, they never actually saw what was happening.

How many organisations do you know of where the directors hold meetings in their offices in big cities where they make decisions affecting the working conditions and lives of employees thousands of miles away?

The Utopian Director makes it their business to constantly walk around all arms of their organisation. The recognise the transformations that occur when organisations like John Deere institute programmes of constant feedback (every two days) to keep senior managers informed and in touch with the mood of employees.

Pause & Meditate on: *What sort of Director am I? Do I care passionately about the organisation's cause? Am I in touch with the thoughts and feelings of all the employees for whom I am responsible?*

15. DIRECTORS AND MANAGERS
HAVE TO BECOME COACHES

D eveloping people, your most valuable asset, has to become a priority of all managers at all levels.

According to a recent Gallup survey 67% of employees who agree the their manager focusses on their strengths are engaged at work. When employees disagree the percentage plummets to just 2%.

16. HOW TO GET QUALITY RESULTS

I believe that people want to do well. They want to produce quality results. The feeling of pride that one experiences when one's original idea is accepted is one of the best feelings that a human being can enjoy. That is why awards ceremonies are so popular. The feeling of pride that is experienced when your team gets a result is one of the feelings that makes life worth living.

The aim of workplace utopia is to allow people to experience that wonderful feeling as often as possible and thereby promote the productivity and growth of their employers organisation.

How is quality work produced in workplace utopia?

1. The right people do jobs that suit their skill sets and allow free rein to their thoughts, ideas and passions. This requires that all people are interviewed to discover their strengths as well as their passions and are then appropriately employed - see Chapter 4 on ikigai.

2. Managers have to create clear and inspiring individual

goals that contribute to the achievement of the corporate goal. These individual goals are created mutually and agreed with each individual responsible for the outcome.

3. People have to be given time, space, facilities and support to do what is required of them. Then they have to be left alone and allowed to get on with their work. This means that they have to *take responsibility* for delivering and managers have to *trust* that they will deliver.

4. The environment of the workplace has to be lively, fun, happy and inspiring - a place where freedom of expression is encouraged.

How can this work?

Managers need to focus primarily on goal setting, motivation and providing regular growth feedback. Managers need to trust their subordinates, rely on the progress reports that are submitted regularly and not keep getting in the way by moving the goal posts and constantly demanding information.

Subordinates need to take responsibility for delivering on their mutually agreed goals. They need to report upwards at agreed intervals on their progress.

Pause and Meditate about: *What do I have to do to create a workplace where each employee gives of their best?*

17. TEAM WORK

F rench agricultural engineer Max Rigelmann discovered in the 19th century that when more people pulled on a rope each individual expended less effort. This suggests that teams that are too large will become less efficient. However, it does not tell us the optimum desirable size for a team.

Looking at the size of sports teams, 5 in basketball, 9 in baseball and 11 in football suggests that the size of the team should be related to the size of the pitch (task) and the amount of time between breaks.

The suggestion here is that the size of the team should be related to the size of the task. But consideration must also be given to the need to divide tasks into manageable chunks.

The aim of all team leaders should be to create synergy within their team. Synergy being the state in which people cooperate together so well that the team's total output is greater than could be expected from the sum of its parts.

Teams with synergy tend to have clear direction, act with

passion, be completely committed and really know their subject. They work as a unit, communicating freely and supporting one another.

How do you create a team with synergy?

* Set a clear goal.

* Gather a group of people who believe passionately that the achievement of the goal will make a worthwhile difference to some aspect of life.

* Get the team to develop the strategy. This should include the time frame for achieving the goal and a budget.

* Agree the strategy with the team and agree how they will keep you informed of their progress. Agree that they will provide you with continuous feedback on the state of each individual's emotional engagement with the strategy.

* Support the team with the facilities that they require.

* Trust the team and get out of their way.

* Take note of the continuous feedback and offer help where needed.

Pause and Meditate about: *Do my teams have synergy? What do I have to do to create synergistic teams?*

18. FEEDBACK

F eedback is the lubricant that oils the wheels of the utopian workplace.

The role of feedback is to help people develop. Feedback should not be used to judge or criticise (unless it is constructive) but rather to open the door to understanding, learning and growth.

Your motto for feedback should be: **"don't judge - teach."**

19. THE UTOPIAN WORKPLACE

What needs to happen for a utopian workplace to exist?

1. Directors need to be clear about their organisation's goal.

2. Directors must create an inspiring mission statement which states what you are passionate about.

3. Directors need to commit to creating a utopian workplace in the full belief that this is the right way to go.

4. Directors need to get the full commitment of other directors to the belief that this is the path to continuous growth and prosperity and high staff engagement.

5. Directors need to become ambassadors for the utopian workplace in order to convince their employees that they are fully committed to this way of being.

6. The Directors' aim should be to create a family atmosphere in which everyone feels stimulated and free to express themselves.

Pause & Meditate on: *Does the idea of a utopian workplace really excite me? Do I fully believe that this is the best way for my organisation to thrive and prosper?*

20. ABOUT THE AUTHOR

David Ferrers is a funder member of Actively Engaged the organisation designed to help employers create work environments where employees are inspired and committed to the corporate goals.

David spent the first part of his career working for some of the world's largest advertising agencies. He has been a full time, professional Personal Development Coach for over a quarter of a century.

David mainly coaches individuals in the corporate sector for multi-nationals such as: Elsevier, P&O, Dell, Xerox, Prudential, GMAC, Yves St.Laurent, Bosch and Axa. He has also worked for British Government departments; The Cabinet Office and Defra.

The author is an NLP Master Practitioner who has written several books on Personal Growth, plus two novels. He helps run Actively Engaged workshops both online and at physical locations

You can find out more about the author at the Actively Engaged website: https://activelyengaged.com

36396307R00039

Printed in Great Britain
by Amazon